DIGGING DEEP
in the garden

BOOK ONE

John Walker

**Winner of the Garden Media Guild
Environmental Award**

Earth-friendly Books
www.earthfriendlygardener.net

For Gaby Bartai

ISBN: 978-0-9932683-3-5

Editor: Gaby Bartai

Cover design by Darren Moseley at www.kablooiecreative.co.uk

First published in the United Kingdom in 2015 (1)

Earth-friendly Books
Snowdonia
North Wales

www.earthfriendlygardener.net

Cover image: bumblebee (*Bombus* sp.) and hoverfly/drone fly (*Eristalis pertinax*) foraging on *Helenium* 'Waltraut'. Cover image © John Walker

CONTENTS

INTRODUCTION

At the start of 2006 I was given an opportunity that changed my gardening as well as my writing life (and life in general, come to think of it). That winter, during a rock-hard freeze, I floated an idea to the then editor of the much-missed *Organic Gardening* magazine, Gaby Bartai, for a column under the tagline 'Digging Deep'. My pitch was to tackle the difficult, mostly unasked questions about how we gardeners (organic or otherwise) relate to wider environmental concerns, and how gardening affects, for good or ill, the living world around us. Gaby took me on, promising her readers that we would 'rattle a few cages', and over the next four and a half years I did my best – with some notable successes – to oblige.

While blowing the dust off these cage-rattling essays and gathering them together for this book, two things struck me. The first is that almost a decade since 'Digging Deep' took root, many of the issues I explored are still getting worse – think climate chaos, pesticide pollution, profligate energy use. And yet gritty garden writing exploring such topics is still almost non-existent; we plod on under the illusion – ably propped up by an out-of-touch media – that gardening and the wild, natural world are somehow opposites, rather than being intimately interwoven.

The second is that many of the questions I asked back then still yearn for answers; brought together here they pack quite a punch. Now more than ever, we gardeners need to ask questions. To quiz, to probe and to challenge gardening's status quo is a gentle yet powerful way of changing things for the better – which is, after all, what gardening at its simplest, its most essential and earth-friendly, is all about.

Don't ever stop digging.

John Walker – Snowdonia, North Wales, Summer 2015

CLIMATE OF DENIAL

BACK IN DECEMBER my garden experienced a few memorably cold days of white-over frost with, on one night, an impressive -9.5°C registering on the outdoor thermometer. I love this kind of genuine winter weather, when the ground turns to rock, and the grip of the season is so tight you wonder how your garden will ever break free. After a run of middle-of-the-road, mild and nondescript winters, frost, snow, freezing fog and plummeting mercury are to be celebrated.

We should cherish these bouts of what we've come to think of as 'real' winter, as well as real spring, summer and autumn weather, because taking even the most dispassionate look at the growing evidence about what future weather patterns might hold, it's clear that each spell of ice-etched winter could be our last. I'm talking, of course, about the potential effects of global, human-induced climate change.

The freeze over, a soggy thaw drove me in from the garden and, flicking through the February 2006 issue of *Gardeners' World* magazine, I happened on an article called 'Changing times'. Billed as a piece '... to help our gardening adapt to the shift in seasons', it sounded interesting, so I read on. My eyes widened with each paragraph and a chill went through my soul. The writer, having dismissed atmospheric warming as being down to little more than 'wobbles' in the earth's axis, declares that, 'In short, climate change is natural. The real news would be if our climatic conditions remained static, but that wouldn't sell newspapers.'

Surely the media can't be to blame for the greatest environmental challenge we've ever faced – but let's not get sidetracked. I was gobsmacked. Apart from the fact that a fellow organic gardener was saying it, it was coming from arguably the nation's most respected and best-known gardener: Alan Titchmarsh.

I find it deeply troubling and verging on the reckless for such a high-profile gardener as Alan to make such a sweeping and dismissive statement. Is he seriously questioning the mounting scientific consensus on man-made climate change? I expect an awful lot better from someone who can, with just a single sentence or sound bite, wield such influence over this gardening nation. And before any Titchmarshophiles start snorting their fury, let me explain why.

As an organic gardener, I care deeply for the earth, but I also care increasingly about the impact – good and bad – of my gardening on the world around me. I didn't used to think like this, and believe me, I wish I didn't have to. One of my most powerful responses to what a climate-uncertain future might hold is an emotional one. The thought of losing those frozen winter days forever fills me with a deep sadness, which deepens further when Alan writes, '... our planet has warmed up before – there were warm tropical periods between the Earth's many ice ages and mini-ice ages, and they happened quite quickly.'

No one would dispute that, but 'quite quickly' is a very relative term, and Alan's argument attempts to use naturally occurring climate change over millennia to normalise human-induced change within decades. I don't want 'quite quickly' hurried along by the release of greenhouse gases and turned into rapid, runaway and unpredictable. I want climate change to be natural, to take aeons and be imperceptible to generations – just as it should be. I don't want snowdrops and frogspawn in autumn, nor am I much fussed about having dahlias flowering in November. As for Alan's 'wetter winters' and 'hotter and drier' summers: no thank you.

Emotional outburst vented, let's get down to some nitty gritty.

Alan's dismissal of climate change as 'natural', and therefore, by implication, nothing to fret about, highlights what is probably, in environmental terms, the fundamental problem with the gardening industry: the almost total, and conveniently maintained, lack of any real connection between gardening and the environment. Yes, there are the familiar, high-profile topics, like the use of peat in composts, that usher us towards a bag of New Horizon, but for many – let's call them the not-yet-organic – the massive environmental benefits of organic gardening remain undiscovered.

So what are these massive benefits? Surely gardening is just a hobby; why should all gardeners be signing up to the environmental cause? The answer is simple: in a world where environmental pressures grow daily, there's a palpable sense of helplessness about what difference we, as individuals, can make. We can do all the recycling and fit the house out with low-energy bulbs – which is laudable – but where we can make a real difference, on so many levels, both locally and globally, is out in our gardens.

Let's tot up what benefits an average, established organic garden, growing vegetables, fruit, herbs and flowers, can bring: self-sufficiency in some food crops; fresh, residue-free produce; not a 'food mile' on the clock; zero packaging, meaning less use of natural and finite resources, and less waste; fewer shopping trips by vehicle, so less burning of fossil fuel and less of a contribution to global warming; no use of synthetic, oil-hungry pesticides; *in situ* recycling of organic matter through composting; a booming garden ecosystem; and the most minimum-impact, maximum-benefit workout for body, mind and soul there is. I'd call that a pretty impressive difference, even if we only achieve some of it.

Further on in Alan's article, there's a glimmer of hope. 'So if we agree the climate is changing, and that we must all do our bit to ensure we don't exacerbate the situation, where does this leave gardeners?' Sadly, what follows is not a call to embrace gardening as an empowering, accessible way of tackling environmental issues, but more debunking of 'the climate change bandwagon' – and a plug for his new TV series and book. He can be forgiven for the latter, but not for his part in a widening of the divide between gardening and our environment – or for encouraging gardeners to sink, like him, into climate change denial.

Alan's opinions are symptomatic of an alarming and growing trend among some garden writers and broadcasters. They peddle the so-called 'benefits' of global warming ('we can grow all those lovely tender plants'), but seem oblivious to the fact that, in many ways, gardening, and the industry supporting it, is actually helping to stoke climate change. This new wave of garden communicators, willing to see climate change as mere opportunity, in print or at the checkout, strike me as being seriously ecologically challenged.

As gardening and the environment become ever more intimate bedfellows, there's a painful rub looming for the gardening industry. As environmental awareness grows, a greater sense of inquiry tends to blossom alongside it. As the powerful, positive effects of organic gardening inspire more of us, we'll become more discerning. We'll pass over peat-based composts without a second thought, start asking awkward questions at the garden centre about the origins and ecological credentials of their wares, and drive the real, long-overdue 'greening' of gardening from the roots up.

And just think: as this unstoppable band of organic gardeners blooms across the land, we might, with any luck, still be able to enjoy the grip of those freezing winter days and these warm, encouraging bursts of spring. Just as nature intended. *April 2006*

GARDENS IN THE AIR

AS I WRITE, the moon floats imperceptibly across a cloudless blue sky. As ever, I'm entranced, wondering if I can really see it move. I can't, of course, but below the moon, I spot something that does. It brings me back to my laptop with a bump – and to the very topic infusing my thoughts on this fine day.

For adorning the sky are the criss-crossing vapour trails – or contrails – of aircraft, which start their brief lives ruler-straight before crumpling before your eyes like worn-out paper chains. It's hard to believe that these transient, beautiful sketches on the sky are also the evidence of humanity's most polluting and ecologically destructive mode of transport.

By the time you read this, the Chelsea Flower Show will be just weeks away. Much of the infrastructure of 'the greatest flower show on earth' will be in place. Countless tons of raw materials, let alone plants, will have been shipped onto the site, using vast amounts of fossil fuel. Yet the energy consumed on the ground will be as nothing compared to the lengths some exhibitors have gone to in order to stage a five-day wonder.

Anyone gardening beneath London's major airport flight paths will already have had some of the show passing, quite literally, overhead. For this year, the Royal Horticultural Society (RHS) – the organiser of Chelsea and most of the other major gardening shows – is boasting not one but two show gardens flown in from the other side of the world.

Fleming's Nurseries, which is staging an 'Australian garden', is a serial offender, having exhibited at Chelsea twice already, but the real eyebrow-raiser this May comes courtesy of Tourism New Zealand's '100 per cent Pure New Zealand Garden'. The press release boasts that, 'Over 1,500 plants are being shipped to the UK, in five airfreight containers,' on top of an equal number being sourced from Europe. Then there's the 'locally sourced' rock, pebbles taken from 'hilltop, river bed and coast', and a good dollop of 'black sand'. All local to *New Zealand*, that is. The plants will be grown in 'four cubic metres of fumigated potting mix' and spend nine weeks in quarantine. On touchdown in the UK they will be grown on at RHS Garden Wisley.

It's arguable that there is nothing inherently wrong with other continents showcasing their gardening expertise; we have all benefitted in different ways. I've been visiting Chelsea for almost 30 years and have enjoyed some sheer spectacles, both home-grown and international, but in those 30 years our ecological awareness has advanced dramatically. Only a hermit will not have heard of human-induced climate change, and we're now warned almost daily by scientists the world over that we may be closer to a 'tipping point' (the point at which our efforts to mitigate further climate change become futile) than ever imagined. So to be flying in gardens, not to mention the people to construct them, from the most distant places on the planet, is simply potty (the same applies to those well-travelled plants and materials that end up in garden centres). Yes, it will fan the fickle flames of the media for a day or two, and massage a few egos, but it will also do its bit for global warming, and send out the message that it's gardening as usual, whatever the environmental cost.

I felt duty-bound to have a root around on the RHS website to get a feel for where the UK's 'leading gardening charity dedicated to advancing horticulture and promoting good gardening' stands on such pressing issues as climate change. At the time of writing there isn't a lot. Granted, there are leaflets on 'use of resources' and 'biodiversity in the garden', which are undoubtedly useful, but there is nothing addressing the big issues of the day, nor anything connecting our desires and actions as gardeners with their impact on the world around us.

Then, on the home page of the site, the headline, 'What cost the world in your garden?' My heart raced. Could this be the RHS reaching its own 'tipping point'? Was this the first step in a long, hard 'roots up' examination of the consequences, for better or worse, of gardening, and the effects of the industries that support it? Was it the opening salvo in a wider debate about the use of natural resources, energy consumption, the role gardening plays in stoking climate change, or how it might be harnessed to help mitigate it? No. This was actually a report from a conference where gardeners, scientists and policy makers discussed whether the increasing international trade in plants posed a risk of importing new pests and diseases.

That conclusion is blindingly obvious, but I checked through the conference summary and found not a single mention of the potentially far more devastating effects of moving plants around the globe by land, sea and air, which involves the guzzling of vast amounts of fossil fuel and the consequent belching of greenhouse gases. Clearly this wasn't the remit of this gathering, but one might hope it would be a topic for discussion. It seems we are content, in Nero-like fashion, to carry on gardening while the world warms, demonstrating the same ecocidal tendency that flies in mangetout from southern Africa in the middle of our winter.

I have no axe to grind with the RHS. I am a member myself and have nothing but admiration for much of what it does to promote gardening. Its power to foster debate and influence thinking is awesome; when I last checked it had 360,000 members and (despite its lukewarm 'policy' on organics) a good number of those, like me, will be gardening organically.

The reason I single it out is precisely because it has such huge potential to influence not only the gardening practices of its members, but of the entire gardening industry, both here in the UK and further afield. It also needs to be kept in the spotlight because it organises, manages and sets policy for most of our major national gardening shows, which, through the media, reach millions worldwide.

So just imagine the consequences of a new raft of review and reform of all the RHS's activities. Imagine a seismic shift in its policy on flower shows, including the banning of show gardens from outside the UK. Gas-guzzling gardens from the other side of the world would stay firmly on the runway, as a new 'sustainable gardening' policy took root at the core of the RHS's work. Discouraging the use of peat at its shows, which is already policy (and fiercely opposed by some), would be but a drop in the garden pond. Those harping for horticultural business as usual, who see nothing but 'opportunities' in climate change, would be swept away by a growing wave of ecologically enlightened gardeners stepping out on a more planet-friendly, organic path.

Will we see more air-freighted gardens touch down at Chelsea next year? Probably. Will the RHS seize the moment and steer the UK's gardeners onto a greener path? Eventually, yes, either through taking the initiative or by bowing to the will of its members. Cynics may well be thinking that pigs might fly. Don't forget that gardens already do. *May 2006*

PLANET PATIO

ANY PASSING OWL would have labelled me the ultimate peeping Tom. It was gone nine o'clock in the evening and the surrounding garden was caught in the spell of a sparkling rime frost, the grass crunching like a carpet of tiny eggshells. And there I was, peering wide-eyed through the hedge at the neighbours, with only starlight to unmask me. Inhaling the crisp air hinted at a temperature heading for -5°C, probably lower.

Now I know it sounds far-fetched, but the reason for this foray into nocturnal voyeurism was that between me and the neighbours there was no glass. They weren't sitting in their living room, or even in their conservatory (though that would have been bad enough). No, they were sitting outside; they were also having a barbecue. This was late November. How, and why?

The answer takes the form of a tall, shiny metallic beast standing around 2.25m (7ft) tall with a cylindrical base and flying saucer-like top. Inside the base is a can of propane gas – the sort campers use. Propane comes from oil and/or natural gas, and is a fossil fuel. Using a 12 kilowatt output model for two hours on its highest setting (essential on a freezing November night) releases around 5.2kg of carbon dioxide (CO_2) – equivalent to that released daily by a car during average use. Carbon dioxide is the most significant of the gases contributing to global climate change.

Most models can accommodate a 13kg gas cylinder, and the government estimates that there are 630,000 of them in use in gardens, with up to 105,000 used in the 'hospitality sector', which boils down mostly to pub gardens (and this is a figure set to rocket in the wake of the smoking bans). You do the sums. Scary, isn't it? Even our MPs are on to this one; questions asked in parliament have revealed that these 'must-have' garden gadgets have increased our emissions of CO_2 in the UK by up to 380,000 tonnes a year. One MP has even suggested they be banned, or at least carry a 'health warning'. As well as contributing directly to potentially catastrophic climate change, the things are grossly inefficient, with most of the heat heading straight into the atmosphere, accompanied by various unfiltered pollutants.

The patio heater has to be one of the most un-green of all the beacons of the 'outdoor living' phenomenon. It was painful enough seeing an immeasurable area of decent, fertile garden soil suffer death by decking in the wake of 'Ground Force', which arguably did more environmental harm than good, despite its bleating that it 'got people out gardening'. Now we want to sit out in our gardens all year round, whatever the weather's doing, and be T-shirt warm to boot.

Some people do, at least. It seems that the frugal instincts of gardeners, especially us organic bunch, are being dwarfed by the prophets of profligacy, who exhibit a growing tendency towards 'season denial'. The garden is an 'extension of the home' and it seems we must treat it – and heat it – accordingly. The neighbours, by the way, now square up to nature regularly, only being forced inside when it pours. Still, back indoors they might just snatch a glimpse on TV of our rapidly melting ice caps.

I'm no killjoy, but I'm all for curtailing our insatiable desire for unchecked pleasure when it's quite literally killing our planet. This is outdoor living gone mad, and I seriously wonder if those living on 'planet patio' actually inhabit the same miraculous orb of interconnected life that I do. The greenest thing I can think of doing when the sun goes down is pulling on a jacket, and when that fails, going indoors. Simple, but entirely profitless – and there's the rub. We're brainwashed by glossy magazines and TV makeovers into 'living' outdoors and, unsurprisingly, we're then handed a bottle of cheap fossil fuel to help us achieve it. Search the internet for patio heaters and the screen is plastered with them, many with prices around £100 and falling. You can't help wondering, with a sense of ecological trepidation, what's next. Now we've a way of heating the patio 365 days a year, all we need is for some bright spark to come up with a way of cooling it down. Funnily enough...

'With world climate change giving us hotter summers, the English garden is becoming more of an extension of the home than ever before. The marketplace has seen a considerable increase in spend by the consumers (*sic*) to make their outdoor space a pleasing environment for entertaining, enjoyment and leisure time. Tropical plants now thrive in this more apt environment and offer glamour to the suburban garden.' Enough. This is the opening shot from a firm encouraging us to start guzzling another natural resource – water.

Apart from being misleading – we may be going to experience colder, wetter summers; no one knows – this is yet another example of the 'gardening' industry cashing in on profligate use of natural resources, while using climate change itself as a selling point – all seductively packaged as another must-have accessory for outdoor living.

'Mistscaping allows for the subtle introduction of fog/mist effects into any outdoor application, creating a relaxing ambience with the dramatic, physical cooling effects created by flash evaporation.' Yes, now we can not only heat up the patio, we can use up precious – and in some areas, such as south-east England, dwindling – resources to cool it down. The mind boggles. This press release arrived within days of the reporting of the results from the first satellite study showing that the Antarctic ice sheet is in 'significant decline', releasing 35 cubic miles of water into the sea each year and helping to raise sea levels globally. So it's a chilling irony, in every sense, that the company peddling 'mistscaping' is called Polar Microclimate (there's even a firm called Arctic selling patio heaters). If hosepipe bans and compulsory water meters don't put a stop to this madness, let's hope common sense will.

But my fear is common sense alone won't be enough, nor will it take hold in time. A peek into the average back garden suggests that many people have become so estranged from nature that the evidence against patio heaters and their ilk, as damning as it is, is falling on deaf ears. Encouraging a new wave of people to step into the 'outdoor room', which should have brought them closer to their gardens, and to nature itself, has backfired. If large numbers of them are prepared to send plumes of carbon dioxide into the air on sub-zero nights, and atomise drinking water into cloud fodder on hot summer days, at a time when awareness of environmental problems has never been greater, what hope can there be of every garden in the land becoming even a little more green?

I might just step up my peeping Tom activities. I'm going to keep peering through hedges, and I might even pluck up the courage to give those grilling themselves under a patio heater an eco-roasting. The first question I'll be asking is, are you living on planet patio, or planet Earth? *June 2006*

GROWING LOUDER

THE NEXT THOUSAND WORDS or so are intended as a rallying cry, an environmental call to arms, if you like, to organic gardeners everywhere. My hope is that at least some of you who choose to read this article will, by the end of it, be moved – if you aren't already – to shout about organic gardening from the rooftops of your sheds, greenhouses and polytunnels.

Environmental issues now infuse all of our media; gone are the days when those chaining themselves to trees in an attempt to thwart another road development made news headlines for only a few fleeting moments. Environmental concerns, especially climate change, are now firmly established as 'big' news, and in recent months the print and broadcast media have been awash with facts, figures, opinions and sometimes fictions about our impending ecological ills. You might think that this bringing of environmental matters to a mass audience can only be a good thing. I for one am not so sure.

To its credit, *The Independent* newspaper keeps a close eye on matters environmental, and on global climate change in particular. This spring it asked its readers to suggest their own ideas for 'saving the planet'. (The replies were forwarded to the All-Party Climate Change Group led by Colin Challen MP, who are arguing that to mitigate global warming, the 'business as usual' attitude will simply not do.) *The Independent* received an 'overwhelming' response, resulting in pages of ideas, suggestions and solutions to help combat climate change. I read, word for word, almost all of the responses published.

On the face of it, this was all good stuff – there can't be many downsides to general awareness-raising about issues likely to directly influence the future unfolding of life on this planet. But as I read about low-energy light bulbs, loft insulation and the need to discourage air travel, it struck me that one vital, supremely positive and planet-enhancing strand to this debate was missing. Gardening, organic or otherwise, was not once posited as a 'planet-saving' measure. There were the predictable references to local organic food production and the resultant reduction in 'food miles', and, encouragingly, a ban on patio heaters made it into the 'top 10' ideas put forward for Earth's salvation – quite right, too.

But the simple act of gardening, of pushing your fingers into the soil, of feeling the sun on your neck, of savouring your own food, or of enjoying a bunch of flowers gathered from your own patch, didn't make *The Independent's* top 10. In fact, it hardly 'made it' at all. Permaculture got a mention, but gardening, not a squeak. We seem to have become fixated on solar panels and wind turbines, getting on our bikes, and searching out goods labelled 'ethical fair-trade local organic', all of which, it seems, will do the much-vaunted 'saving'. Doubtless they'll do their bit, but we seem to have lost sight of the simpler things we can do, which involve taking, in most cases, only a few footsteps outdoors. Gardening seems to have disappeared from the environmental radar.

Part of the reason for this lies with the media itself; if you tell people often enough that low-energy light bulbs, loft insulation and not leaving electrical appliances on stand-by are planet-saving measures, the idea will take root and grow into positive action that becomes second nature. Perhaps this is inevitable; we all switch on lights daily, but not everyone gardens. We all use electrical appliances of some kind, but we don't all spend that much of our time outdoors.

As a writer, I'm inherently interested in communication, and I find one of the best settings for explaining ideas, answering questions and making all kinds of different connections is in my garden. When I tell visitors that I have never had, nor ever will have, a wheelie bin here, their reactions range from raised eyebrows to thinly veiled suspicion; some cannot believe such a thing possible. When I moved here, there was no wheelie bin, and as time passed, the need for one never arose, largely due to my obsessive penchants for recycling, composting and making minimal-waste shopping choices. When the very thought of life without a big plastic 'guilt gobbler' sends a flicker of terror over visitors' faces, I take them swiftly to my compost bin, and off comes the lid.

As they peer in, their terror-stricken looks are replaced by curiosity and quiet amazement, for my bin contains anything with even an outside chance of being transformed into compost: kitchen scraps, scrunched paper and cardboard, food packaging, used kitchen towels, and the contents of hoover bags, as well as weeds, fallen leaves, pulled-up bracken and other organic waste gathered from the garden itself. A handful of this 'work in progress', dug carefully from the beating heart of the bin, reveals a tangle of brandling worms thrashing amid the crumbling remains of a cornflake packet.

Easing up the base of the bin, I can tease out a handful of rich, black compost, which I proffer for a 'sniff test'. I then point out the decent growth on the first soft fruit to benefit from this compost in my still fledgling garden. Birds permitting, I'll be picking my first harvest of black, red and whitecurrants this summer, and I can weave into that moment a tale of zero packaging, food footsteps instead of miles, and how there's not a drop of pesticide residue in sight.

All of this – the glee with which I announce my sans-wheelie status, the pride with which I pull the lid off my compost bin, and the sheer delight of sharing my first ripe blackcurrants – is about making connections. I can talk about minimising personal waste through careful purchasing decisions, then seeing just how much unavoidable packaging I can turn into compost to reduce my contribution to landfill. This leads me on to discussing different approaches to composting, and then showing off the results. I can then demonstrate the effect of using that compost, my audience's taste-buds being judge and jury. And when you've taken only a few footsteps to harvest produce, the full ecological insanity of global food miles suddenly hits home hard.

If I were asked to rank everyday activities for their 'environmental connectivity factor', organic gardening would go to the top of my list. There is simply no better place in which to engage others in the widening environmental debate than slap bang in the middle of your own garden. My 'call to arms' urges you to do just one thing: throw open your garden gate this summer and let people in. Let them see for themselves what organic gardening is all about, talk to them, engage with them, and start making compelling connections. In these times of ecological uncertainty, our gardens can and must become powerful and persuasive players in the environmental debates ahead.

It would be wonderful to think, next time a national newspaper asks its readers for their planet-saving suggestions, that its pages might bloom with a whole crop of interconnected ideas courtesy of us organic gardeners. But for that to happen, we all need to start gardening louder. *July 2006*

CONNECTION FAILURE

I'M A BULLY; A THUG, EVEN. I'm not the meek, mild and increasingly environmentally savvy organic gardener I thought I was; I now, apparently, display the most despicable of all human traits. This has crept up on me by stealth, and I didn't even know it had happened until quite recently. Not until I read it in a national newspaper, that is.

The point is that I am not a bully by nature. What I am – in equal measure, I feel – is both organic gardener and environmentalist. For me the two are increasingly entwined. But there's the rub: it seems you are no longer allowed to be a gardener and an environmentalist, for the latter is becoming an increasingly dirty word in some gardening circles, and in some 'mainstream' gardening magazines. So although I consider myself a gardener, with my fingers firmly in the soil, the fact that I also consider myself an environmentalist earns me the label of bully. I must get the cap.

Earlier this year, a climate change activist for the Green Party caused feathers to fly in both the gardening and the national press by suggesting that the emissions from petrol-driven lawnmowers are 'extremely high' and are contributing to global warming. It was suggested that gardeners should ask themselves if mowing their lawn was absolutely necessary, and that they should switch to using electric lawnmowers (preferably using electricity from a renewable source). Other credible ideas put forward (some were less so) included the most eco-friendly mowing solution of all –

using a push mower.

The Green Party has germinated a debate on what must be, alongside the use of patio heaters, one of gardening's most direct contributions to greenhouse gas emissions. Yet the response in some gardening magazines and newspapers left me dumbfounded – not least because I only then discovered that I was a bully.

At the end of April, *The Daily Telegraph* reported on the Green Party's suggestions, canvassing comment from various 'experts', among them celebrity gardener Anne Swithinbank, a panellist on BBC Radio Four's 'Gardeners' Question Time'. She was quoted as follows, "These environmentalists should stop bullying gardeners. They obviously think we are a soft touch but they should be looking at the problems of cheap air flights and emissions from planes. Gardeners don't go jetting off on frequent foreign holidays. They are much too busy in their gardens where they are doing much less harm to the environment." These comments struck me as naive and probably drafted on the back of a seed packet; they also set in motion the divergence of my personality between 'soft touch' and bully.

What Anne's comments starkly demonstrate is the almost total lack of 'joined-up gardening' from an increasing number of celebrity gardeners and the publications they beam out from. In citing 'cheap air flights and emissions from planes', Anne put not one fork tine but all four straight through her foot. Flicking through the May 2006 issue of *The Garden*, the Royal Horticultural Society journal, I find no less than five full-page adverts for overseas gardening holidays, virtually all requiring air travel. (It should be said that *The Garden* is by no means unique in this.) They may not be 'cheap' flights, but some are very long, and the damaging emissions are there regardless. So much for gardeners not 'jetting off'.

Anne Swithinbank features regularly in *Amateur Gardening*, a celebrity-addicted weekly magazine. Its reporting, in its 20th May 2006 issue, of the Green Party's concerns over lawnmowers, raises even more cause for concern. Its news editor's comment begins, 'Environment campaigners appear to be bored with targeting users of peat and patio heaters. Now they've set their sights on petrol mowers, which according to the Green Party, cause 100 per cent more pollution than modern cars.' By now I was confused; was I the bully, the bullied, or somehow both? It continued, 'Mowers help us maintain a pleasant environment. Over 70 per cent of the UK's mowers run on electricity. And if everyone chucked out their petrol mowers, it would send a huge amount of waste to polluting landfill sites.'

What message is this sending out? Does this mean that gardeners are 'targets' for anyone concerned with the effect we are having on our planet's fragile ecosystem, and that environmentalists are fickle enough to switch topics when one runs cold? If just the former is true, then by rights I should, extraordinarily, have myself in my own sights. Suffice to say that the negative impact of peat extraction and, more recently, the use of patio heaters, is beyond question – and it seems to have passed *Amateur Gardening* by. As for portraying environmentalists as fickle, nothing could be more wrong. The truth is that the seed of environmentalism is found in all gardeners. In some it still lies dormant, in others it's already blossoming into positive action.

What lies at the nub of the hare-brained comments in *Amateur Gardening* is, I suspect, this. If you keep gardening and 'the environment' well apart, all will be well; gardeners can be portrayed as 'victims' being bullied by nasty environmentalists, and your magazine can 'defend' you while it keeps on carrying advertisements for peat-based composts, patio heaters and yes, you guessed it, lawnmowers. As for the red herring of the 'huge amount' going to landfill, most petrol mowers are made largely of easily recycled metal. Ironically it's the cheap, mass-produced electric versions which are likely to end up languishing underground (not that the manufacturers will be complaining).

The alternative to this desperate scramble to be seen

championing the gardener's cause, while not rocking the advertising boat, is to encourage those seeds of environmental concern to germinate in all of us – to start explaining the huge positive benefits that gardening, especially organically, can bring.

At the heart of that process lies the need for us to drastically reduce our wolfing of the earth's finite natural resources, with peat and fossil fuels at the top of the list. But it goes much further. It involves taking stock of how we currently garden, and finding better ways of doing things that won't cost us the earth on which all life depends. Just imagine these kind of sentiments appearing in mainstream gardening magazines; we would, in a very short time, see a paradigm shift in the psyche of gardeners everywhere. If magazines then printed, or celebrities came out with, the kind of naive 'opinions' we've seen of late, enthusiasm for both would wilt rapidly.

So don't be bullied into being cast as a 'victim' by magazines or gardening celebrities. Remember that by gardening organically you're already an environmental champion, even if you don't crow about it. And should anyone try to force you to choose between your garden and the fragile world around us, tell them, with a smile, that you're an envirogardener. *August 2006*

COMING OUT ON CLIMATE CHANGE

IMAGINE THIS: you turn on the radio and hear a weedkiller-happy panellist on 'Gardeners' Question Time' being challenged by one of their fellow experts. And I mean challenged, not the usual innocuous banter, descending into a fit of giggles, while the millions listening prepare to slip quietly outside to douse their plots in glyphosate weedkiller (no one really made a fuss about using it, and they're the experts, so it must be OK). Or imagine switching on the television to find two of the presenters of 'Gardeners' World' close to fisticuffs, one making an impassioned case for letting nature attend to pests and diseases, the other armed and ready with the chemical sprayer.

How refreshing that would be. Just imagine the benefits it would bring: a massive increase, virtually overnight, in the level of awareness of organic gardening, coupled with a far more informed debate about how non-organic gardening impacts on the world around us. We might even get a sensible discussion on global warming, instead of the usual twaddle about how wonderful it will be to grow our own olives.

These two programmes alone have a loyal audience of millions, with huge potential to influence the gardening grey matter of our nation. But what would it take to bring about a Damascene conversion among our current crop of high-profile radio and TV gardeners, with their wishy-washy 'I only spray when I have to' approach, or the rather sly 'occasional chemical intervention helps to keep your plants 'healthy'' stance? Arguably, some are already on the road to Damascus, but they really need to get a move on; it is no good saying, "I am totally organic elsewhere in my garden, but I do use one application of combined lawn weedkiller and fertiliser dressing...", as one celebrity gardener did recently – a sop to the garden chemical manufacturers if ever there was one. Perhaps what our celebrity gardeners need – apart from some more gumption – is a role model, someone trusted implicitly, whose TV programmes attract audiences in excess of all of their own shows gathered together. Well, I think they have their man: Sir David Attenborough.

Back in May, in an interview with *The Independent*, Sir David said this about climate change. "I'm no longer sceptical. Now I do not have any doubt at all. I think climate change is the major challenge facing the world. I have waited until the proof was conclusive that it was humanity changing the climate. The thing that really convinced me was the graph connecting the increase in carbon dioxide in the environment and the rise in temperature, with the growth of human population and industrialisation." He went on to explain why it had taken him many years, and several ground-breaking TV series, to end his silence on climate change. "People say, everything will be all right in the end. But it's not the case. We may be facing disasters on a global scale." Now that Sir David has 'come out' on climate change, it's high time trusted gardening celebrities followed suit.

Although Sir David's declaration will have a valuable and positive influence on our collective consciousness, he also referred to the helplessness felt by many people. But as gardeners, especially organic gardeners, we have the means to vanquish such helplessness, and a golden opportunity exists for our celebrity gardeners to show the way. In terms of helping to stem global warming and lightening our load on the planet, organic gardeners are uniquely placed to take direct, meaningful action. We just need to carry on doing what we're doing.

By gardening organically (and I mean organically, not the

watered-down version), we're making a bold statement of our environmental and, if you like, ecological intent. Gardening organically shows an understanding of natural processes, of our interaction with, and place in, the natural order of things. It fosters a feeling of respect for the planet and for its inhabitants, encourages us to tread more lightly on the earth, and engenders a powerful sense of self-reliance. Just imagine hearing those last three sentences on your radio, or watching a TV presenter talking like this, with real verve, into the camera.

But, you might be thinking, don't we already have high-profile celebrity organic gardeners, namely Monty Don, lead presenter on 'Gardeners' World', and 'Gardeners' Question Time' panellist Bob Flowerdew? Yes we do, and their espousal of organics is a fantastic and vital contribution, but what's needed now is an upping of the ante to engage gardeners, of every hue, in the widening environmental debate. Monty Don has written passionately about the reality of climate change – but the greatest and fastest change in attitudes will come through the power of mass media, namely radio and television.

People like Sir David Attenborough can help us see the bigger picture, bring the strands together and raise our awareness, but what they can't do is beam a positive message into millions of homes, week in, week out, during our favourite gardening programmes. No one is going to get us thinking about how easy it is to eliminate 'food miles' by growing our own, or how we can create vibrant, pesticide-free gardens by engaging positively with nature, quite like a celebrity gardener who has come out on environmental issues, especially climate change. What we need now is gardening celebrities with insight and courage, who aren't afraid to ask difficult questions, either of their fellow experts or of the gardening industry. We need them to explain the impact, good and bad, of gardening on the world around us, and to make the connections real and relevant.

We need them to demonstrate how gardening other than

organically is redundant and discredited, and how the use of pesticides (even 'selectively') is detrimental both to us and to the other myriad life forms with which we share this planet. They need to remind us of the destructive power of peat extraction, and the barminess of sitting under energy-guzzling patio heaters in mid-winter. They should be bold enough to highlight the vast amounts of waste spewing out of garden centres, and encourage us to question the huge number of 'garden centre miles' being clocked up globally. They could get us all thinking ethically when it comes to garden purchases, not just in choosing peat-free compost, but in, for instance, asking for evidence that that gorgeous patio planter has not been made by child labour in some far-off land. The possibilities are endless.

It might sound like a tall order, but it would have a profound effect on the nation's gardeners – and on the ecology of their gardens. Celebrities can initiate shock waves and bring about radical change – look at Jamie Oliver and school dinners. There's no reason why an influential organic gardener couldn't do the same in the gardening world. They could trigger a revolution in truly sustainable gardening that would see pesticides gathering dust on the garden centre shelves, and put paid to peat-based composts once and for all. As more of us rejoined with nature, helplessness would be replaced by hope as it dawned on us that where we really can 'do our bit', where we can make a real, tangible difference as individuals, is on our balconies and patios, in our gardens, and out on our allotments.

All we need now is our own Sir David.

September 2006

ORGANIC GARDENING: THE END?

ORGANIC GARDENERS who have the misfortune to live next to non-organic farmland will be familiar with the following scenario. There you are, in summer, out in your garden, tending crops into which you have poured time, energy, enthusiasm – and love. Your patch of earth is buzzing with life, and there's an almost palpable sense of ecological equilibrium about you. A sense of balance, of harmony. Then a dirty great tractor rumbles past, belching a cloud of pesticide 'drift' that seeps into every corner of your plot.

If you're gardening in a town or city, there's a shred of comfort to be had knowing that spray drift rarely reaches that far – yet the same thing happens if you have a trigger-happy gardening neighbour who's intent on implementing a policy of 'if it moves, kill it'. In neither case is there any legal requirement for you to be told just what it is that is contaminating your home-grown food.

It's a situation that's as ghastly as it is outrageous, yet it happens to large numbers of gardeners (of whatever ilk) each year. But something even more outrageous and, in organic gardening terms, catastrophic is on the horizon. Yet you won't even know if and when this contamination has taken place. It won't be announced by a thundering tractor, or by your neighbour's frenzied pumping of his garden sprayer.

No, this all-pervasive, insidious contamination will be borne on the breeze, or carried on the wings of innocents such as bees. This contamination has no smell, nor will you be able to see it. This contamination is microscopic, and it comes in the form of grains of pollen. Nothing unusual about that, you might think, except that this pollen has come from plants which have been genetically modified (GM). It's not that long ago that an overwhelming consensus in the UK rejected the prospect of GM food derived from any vegetable, animal or other source. But the spectre of GM crops being grown here in the UK, within the next few years, is again casting a long shadow over our gardens and allotments.

In July, the Department for Environment, Food and Rural Affairs (DEFRA) published its 'Consultation on proposals for managing the coexistence of GM, conventional and organic crops'. This 92-page document (covering England only; other countries will follow) is available to anyone who wishes to comment on the somewhat dubious concept of 'coexistence' with GM crops (which so far include potatoes, maize, sugar beet and oilseed rape). The document concerns itself only with field-scale crop production; gardeners, organic or otherwise, don't even get a look in. And why should they? After all, we're only growing healthy food, incurring minimal or zero 'food miles' and, by gardening organically, collectively contributing incalculable environmental benefits.

In a nutshell, the proposals would allow for non-GM crops – including those we grow in our gardens – to be routinely contaminated by pollen from GM crops. The consultation seeks views on what measures are needed to allow GM crops to 'coexist' with conventional and organic crops, and on who is liable when farmers suffer economic damage due to GM contamination. Most worryingly, it is not asking how non-GM crops can be protected from GM contamination – because the government assumes that significant levels of contamination are acceptable. Indeed, environment minister Ian Pearson has said, "We should not kid ourselves that levels of nought or 0.1% [GM contamination] are either practical or realistic."

Under European food labelling rules, 'accidental' contamination by GM material of up to 0.9% is allowed before food must be labelled as GM. Organisations such as the Soil Association and Friends of the Earth are drawing attention to the fact that the government has taken this to mean that 0.9% contamination in conventional, and possibly in organic, crops is acceptable. Again, all this relates to commercial crops. Who is looking after the interests of us organic gardeners, whose myriad patches of home-grown food surely deserve the same, if not greater, protection?

Certainly not the mainstream gardening press. At the time of writing I have not seen a mention in any other gardening magazine of the effects the growing of GM crops in the UK would have on our gardening nation – practically, emotionally or spiritually. But that's no surprise; some of our gardening industry's most vocal mouthpieces are aggressively pro-GM, believing that glow-in-the-dark roses, or evergreen lawns which don't need mowing, are gardening's final frontier.

Another proposal in the government's consultation concerns so-called 'separation distances' – minimum permitted distances between a GM and non-GM crop, which determine the level of likely contamination; the shorter the distance, the higher the contamination level. As an example, 110m (362ft) is proposed as the minimum separation distance between a crop of GM maize for human consumption and any adjacent non-GM crop of maize for human consumption. But what happens if I am growing sweet corn a stone's throw from a field of GM maize? The pollen of sweet corn/maize is airborne (that's why we tap the male flowers to disperse it), and it can travel for miles on the wind. I haven't a cat in hell's chance of remaining uncontaminated. And as for percentage contamination...

'If GM crops are grown commercially in the UK it will change the nature of the world we live in overnight,' says Susan Kay-Williams, Chief Executive of Garden Organic, the UK's leading organisation for organic gardeners, which is currently formulating its response to the proposals. 'A bee does not know which flower to go to to avoid pollinating a non-GM flower with pollen from a

GM plant. Like the wind, which carries airborne pollen over huge distances, insects don't observe 'no-fly' zones. If contamination from GM crops becomes a reality, we face a grave threat to both our vegetable heritage and to biodiversity in general.'

I've always believed that being able to grow my own food was up there among the most inalienable of human rights. It seems I am wrong, and that even the most basic right – being able to feed myself on food that's free from any kind of contamination – could soon be quashed.

The outcome of this consultation, if it should open the door for the growing of GM crops in the UK, will have profound consequences. It will fundamentally change the way we perceive what drives us to garden organically. It's possible, by taking extreme measures – such as moving house – to escape spray drift, but we can't escape the pervasiveness of GM pollen on the wind. There will simply be nowhere to escape to. Yes, the garden might look much as it ever did, but we will know, deep down, that it's not the same; that that patch of earth we felt was sacrosanct, is no longer so. From then on, there will be no such thing as organic gardening. *October 2006*

GREAT EXPECTATIONS

I'M GOING TO BRAG – about my compost heaps. The one I made recently is something to behold; perfectly round in shape, just the right level of compaction, and ample moisture to kick-start the miraculous process that is 'hot' composting. Within a few days of building you could see steam rising from the top – spectacular illuminated by torchlight on a chilly night – while the metal rod pushed into its core to monitor the temperature was hot enough to singe your skin.

This was some heap, 1.5m (5ft) across and around 1.2m (4ft) deep. Cutting the bracken and the grass, using a scythe, took a good half-day. Collecting together the materials (I 'imported' some bales of old mouldering straw) and then wetting them as the heap went together was another half day's work. All in, building it took a long, full day with a short lunch and scarce tea breaks.

If you think it sounds like a lot of hard work, you'd be right – it was. At the end of my composting sessions, I feel physically exhausted. I've certainly sweated buckets, and when I first started experimenting with these big heaps, at times I was close to tears. But I get a real buzz out of it.

I'm making a new, terraced garden, on a rough, bracken-infested slope. The soil has good structure, but contains virtually no major nutrients, and the pH is 5.1. It desperately needs an avalanche of compost, plus some lime and other minerals. I don't have any manure available locally, so I'm making compost from what I do have plenty of – bracken. And I'm using 'hot' heaps not to kill pests, diseases and weed seeds, but to speed things up.

The sooner I improve my soil and start growing edible crops, the sooner I can go 'food mile neutral'. For me, growing my own food and aspiring to self-sufficiency is as good as it gets, at an individual level, in terms of environmental sustainability and 'doing my bit'.

But even with readily available supplies of organic matter to hand, making a garden on even a modest scale is, at least to start with, hard physical work.

Imagine my incredulity, after staggering in from one of my 'compostathons' to plonk down with a cup of tea and a magazine, when I saw screaming out from its front cover 'Bumper crops, zero effort', 'The 20-minute allotment' and, wait for it, '6 easy ways to make your own compost'. All this was being peddled by a magazine allegedly about 'growing your own'. The subtext read something like this: gardening is easy, quick and effortless. My aching back, sweaty armpits and blistered palms begged to differ.

For at least the last decade, we have been living in the illusory age of so-called 'easy gardening'. We've been sold, through spin and the gardening industry's hunger for profit, the message that gardening requires next to no effort. And it does, superficially, seem that way.

Most TV gardening programmes reinforce the 'maximum results for minimal effort' message. What viewer would imagine that the BBC 'Gardeners' World' garden has a full-time head gardener and a team of staff getting everything ready for the few hours when the presenters descend for filming and make it all look so, well, easy. A 30-minute slot following someone building a compost heap, or digging over an allotment, isn't going to boost the ratings. (The flip side is that 'reality gardening' shows are therefore unlikely to invade our homes and infect our collective consciousness.)

What's desperately needed is a reality check. Perhaps the recent closure of *BBC Easy Gardening* magazine due to falling sales heralds the beginning of a more realistic and honest approach. Books, magazines and TV and radio broadcasts might then show us the way back to what gardening is and always has really been about: intermittent hard work with, especially if you garden organically, priceless rewards.

But the road back to reality, and to giving new gardeners practical and honest advice, will also require a shift in expectations. At the moment we're being told that gardening can be practically instantaneous – 'the 20-minute allotment'. Perhaps if you're growing mustard and cress, or baby salad leaves, it is pretty 'instant', but such examples are few and far between. Honesty, as ever, makes a lousy sound bite.

Recently, as an 'expert' guest on a regional radio programme, I explained that creating a new organic garden is not something to be done in an afternoon, after a trip to the garden centre. As I waxed about how it can take several years to build a garden's ecosystem, and to put nature's checks and balances in place, and warned that new gardeners should expect some disappointments and failures along the way, I could hear the presenters' blank looks. The same reaction greeted my suggestion that the first step in 'going organic' on a new allotment might be to give nature a head start by installing a pond slap bang in the middle of it.

The distorted expectation that gardens can be 'made' in an afternoon has been nurtured alongside the myth of 'easy' gardening. They serve neither gardener nor planet, and I sense that it's only now that we're starting to see the inevitable fallout. Imagine for a moment that you know nothing about gardening, about how to make or nurture a garden, but that your enthusiasm to get going, organically, is uncontainable – and you've been seduced by the promise of those 'bumper crops' for 'zero effort'. You then set about tackling your back garden jungle, or wilderness allotment, quickly realising that 'zero effort' exists only in the wild fantasies of magazine editors. And when you do win over a patch of earth to sow or plant into, it soon dawns that you've become the hero of every lurking slug and snail…

So what happens next? The steely and determined will curse their delusory magazines, get a quick reality check, and keep at it, not compromising on their reasons for going organic in the first place. Others will flounder, ditch their dreams of being organic as 'too much hard work', and reach for the weedkiller, slug pellets and sprayer, lured on by persuasive 'experts' telling them that chemicals are 'good for plants' health'. Some will give up completely, their dream of cutting 'food miles' consigned to the scrap heap labelled 'easy, quick and effortless'.

The serious worry, at a time when sales of vegetable seeds and fruit plants is rocketing, when there are ever-lengthening waiting lists for allotments, and more people than ever are 'growing their own', is that only a minority will prove resolute enough to start, and stay, organic. We risk a whole disillusioned generation becoming addicted to weedkillers and pesticides, at a time when we face environmental meltdown, simply because the 'easy, quick and effortless' dream they were seductively sold turned out to be a total dud.

Back to reality, I'm off to give my compost heap, which is now cooling rapidly, its first turn, ready for its second 'burn'. Time for some hard work. *November 2006*

A DEEPER SHADE OF GREEN

'THERE ARE TWO TYPES of captive bolt pistol: penetrative and non-penetrative. Penetrative stunners drive a bolt into the skull and cause unconsciousness both through physical brain damage and the concussive blow to the skull. The bolt on a non-penetrative stunner is 'mushroom-headed' and impacts on the brain without entering the skull. Unconsciousness is caused by the concussive blow. Traditionally, animals are stunned before their throats are cut but the stun does not actually kill the animal. Animals die from loss of blood after their throats are cut.' This is a quote from the website of Vegetarians International Voice for Animals, or VIVA! (www.viva.org.uk).

As is this: 'The electric waterbath is widely used to stun chickens, turkeys, ducks and geese. Birds are shackled upside down on a moving conveyor which carries them to an electrified waterbath into which their heads are supposed to be immersed. The shackles contact a bar which is connected to earth... with the aim of ensuring that birds suffer a cardiac arrest and die when they enter the waterbath.' The VIVA! website explains just what happens when these and other slaughtering techniques fail to work. It is not for the faint-hearted.

It all sounds grisly, gruesome and downright cruel, and is probably as far removed from the peaceful pleasures of organic gardening as you could ever get. Yet if you're expecting a delivery of steaming farmyard manure this autumn, if you swear by pelleted poultry manure, or regularly use bonemeal or hoof and horn, you are, whether through ignorance or indifference, party to the practices described above. Most of us have never been inside a slaughterhouse, but it does not take much imagination. The activities VIVA! describes are a fact of everyday life in our food industry. And another fact of life is our long-established use, as gardeners, of the by-products of that industry.

As organic gardeners we care deeply for the natural systems around us, of which we are part. We work with nature, not against it, to create healthy, biologically diverse and balanced ecosystems within our gardens and allotments. We recycle feverishly and shun synthetic pesticides. We get a buzz not just from the beneficial insect life we draw to our plots, but from the feeling that what we do has an ethical dimension; it's an inherently 'good thing'. But how many of us, wrapped in the pungent steam rising from a barrowful of manure, have stopped to consider the less ethical side to what we do?

Happily, a new way of growing is emerging that frees us from garden-scale ethical dilemmas. It is a way of growing that breaks our deep-seated reliance on animal by-products, be it their waste materials, ground-up parts of their carcasses, or the blood that flowed through their veins. It's still organics, but with added ethics. It has the potential to turn our gardens an even deeper shade of green, to make them more compassionate, and to change the way we think about the world and our place in it. And you thought organic gardening was already powerful stuff.

Last August, along with other members of the Vegan-Organic Network, I visited Sow & Grow Organics, a youthful 2.5-acre market garden run by Jenny Hall and Keith Griggs, just north of St Helens in Merseyside. Most of the 60-plus types of vegetable, grown both outdoors and in a polytunnel, supply their vegetable box scheme. It currently has 33 customers, 95% of whom live within a two-mile radius of the holding. How's that for low food miles? All vegetable wastes are composted on site; there's a wildlife-rich pond and flower-rich 'beetle banks', and extensive use is made of mulches and a miscellany of green manures. The crops, despite a challenging growing season, were visibly thriving.

Remarkably, all of this is achieved with zero animal inputs: no manure of any kind, nor any 'organic' fertilisers derived from the bodies of animals. Even plant-raising composts are free of animal by-products. This growing system is known as 'vegan-organic' or 'stockfree-organic', signifying that soil fertility is maintained without the need for livestock. It is also a 'closed' system, meaning that virtually all of the fertility required to grow crops is generated within the holding, largely from composted plant wastes and the effective use of green manure crops, deployed via a carefully planned nine-year crop rotation. Green manures are well known to many organic gardeners, but we have as yet only scratched the surface of their potential to build fertility and generally enhance our garden ecosystems. At Sow & Grow we saw sweet corn undersown with buckwheat, its deep roots quietly building fertility, while its flowers were alive with hoverflies and other beneficial insects. Put simply, green manures create fertility for free by trapping sunlight and building biomass. This is returned to the soil to help form humus. We should rename them 'fertility-building crops'.

Demand is growing for food which is certified organic and which is, in addition, grown without any animal inputs – food, if you like, with impeccable moral credentials. Jenny and Keith are among the pioneers of this new approach to feeding ourselves. With fellow stockfree-organic pioneer Iain Tolhurst, Jenny has co-authored the recently published *Growing Green: Organic Techniques for a Sustainable Future*, the world's first handbook for growers and farmers wanting to produce more compassionate organic food. Every organic gardener should read it.

As a long-time, occasionally faltering vegetarian with vegan leanings, I have not yet resorted to using any animal inputs in my new garden. This, I admit, grew more out of local necessity than a desire to avoid the lurking spectre of the slaughterhouse trade (sheep don't do steaming manure heaps). Instead, I am composting like mad and topping up with soil improver from a local composting project. When it comes to adding major plant nutrients, of which my soil has virtually none, I now find myself passing over the 'classic' organic animal-derived fertilisers in favour of their more 'ethical' equivalents. Being vegetarian, I know that I am guilty of inherent hypocrisy in that I still eat a few animal products, knowing full well that those animals, even if organically reared, are still unlikely to see out their days in sun-soaked retirement.

It would be naive to think that if all gardeners gave up using animal by-products, fewer animals would have a penetrative stunner entering their skulls. But it still feels good to know I am on course to create a garden that has not relied in any way on distant, unseen slaughter. And it's not hard to see how, by taking this final step and declaring our gardens 'animal by-product-free zones', we are gardening to an even higher set of values. *December 2006*

TIME TO POWER DOWN?

FOR THE YOUNGEST to the oldest gardener, the novice to the expert, one captivating, enduring and miraculous activity shines out: growing plants from seed. When you stop to ponder how those piles of pumpkins, heavy bunches of carrots, or basketfuls of ripe tomatoes all start out as seeds, the realisation is humbling. When we sow seeds, the worst we can expect if things go wrong and the seeds fail to germinate is disappointment. We can try again and hope for better luck, but life goes on. In some parts of the world, if seeds fail to germinate, or crops fail to establish, those that sowed them could face death.

A United Nations report, prepared for the international climate change talks held in Nairobi in November 2006, warns that Africa will be hit hardest by the effects of climate change being stoked by 'ballooning carbon emissions' from Western nations. It predicts that large cities could disappear as sea levels rise by up to 95cm (3ft 1in) during the next hundred years, that 40% of wildlife habitats could be lost, and that crop yields, already desperately low, could fall by another 5%. Up to 70 million people could be at risk from rising sea levels. Some 70% of people across Africa, and almost 90% of the poor, work in agriculture; if their seeds don't come up, they don't nip to the garden centre for another packet – they start living on food aid.

The prospect of having to rely on what your own garden or allotment produces, for your very survival, ought to send a shudder down the spine of even an expertly 'self-sufficient' gardener. Can you begin to imagine watching your seedlings wither and die, in the sure knowledge that sometime soon you will be relying on food handouts? And will you entertain the thought that, in order to give your own seeds the best start in life, you might actually be condemning fellow 'gardeners' in other parts of the world to a life of grim dependency – or worse? Hence the terrible irony writ large across the front cover of a magazine here on my desk: 'Greenhouse heating: What is the true cost of protecting your crops?' The actual title of the article is equally ironic: 'Heating: A high price to pay?'

Predictably, the article is actually a consideration of the different fuels available for running propagators and heating greenhouses – electricity, gas and paraffin, all of which release carbon dioxide, either through their generation or when they are burnt, as gas and paraffin are, at the point of use. The main focus of the article is on the costs of using different fuels and the types of heater available. A few brief paragraphs at the end do discuss being 'environmentally friendly', with the admission that to be completely 'green' you shouldn't really heat a greenhouse at all.

The carbon dioxide produced by a gas- or paraffin-fired heater is a 'greenhouse gas' in every sense. It respects no international boundaries; heating your greenhouse contributes directly to the global 'greenhouse effect'. We can no longer afford to count just the economic cost of nurturing our treasured seeds or cuttings – we need to turn the price tag over and look at the environmental and human costs.

I haven't used a heated propagator, or heated a greenhouse other than to give minimal frost protection *in extremis*, for years. Nor does it worry me that I may never do so again. It's bad news, I know, for the manufacturers of greenhouse gardening equipment, but business as usual, even in the multi-million-pound gardening industry, cannot continue. It would be good news for the planet, and it might just help ease the burden on those who depend on their 'gardening' to stay alive.

If you really can't resist the urge to twiddle the thermostat dial in the coming months, at least keep it at minimum, turn it off when possible, and switch, if you're using electricity, to a renewable supplier. This will at least help us, here in the 'energy-obese' developed world, to tighten our belts. Better still, forget energy-intense artificial heating and make better use of what warm places you already have, or cut to the chase and tap directly into the sun.

One of the most effective 'propagators' I've used, powered entirely by natural and renewable energy, is an empty compost bag turned inside out, so the heat-absorbing black side faces out. I simply slip trays or pots of seeds inside it and stand them on the sunny bench of an unheated greenhouse, polytunnel or lean-to, or in a sunny porch. Failing that, commandeer a sunny window-sill, or use a sheltered south- or west-facing wall or window-ledge. The sun will do the rest, even on cloudy but otherwise bright spring days. Simpler still, slit the bag open and lay it over your sown containers, black side up. Go put your hand into an empty inside-out bag on a sunny day and feel what I mean.

Don't expect the same results you would get from using a heated propagator, or by heating a greenhouse to maintain a constant temperature. It will generally take longer for the seeds to come up, but come up they will. On colder nights it might be necessary to take them indoors, or to be creative with layers of fleece, cardboard and old curtains. If you're using a lean-to greenhouse, even a modest one, think about painting the area of wall it covers black. This will absorb the sun's energy during the day, then act as even more of a 'radiator' at night, especially if it's draped in warm layers on cold nights. Switching on to sunshine, while it might not be as constant as the power flowing through a three-pin plug, or hissing from a gas bottle, costs nothing. Not even lives.

As we consider switching off our propagators and heaters, as we think long and hard about 'powering down' our garden energy use in general, we need to throw another important switch to 'on', and that's a switch in our wider thinking. We need to stop trying to beat or 'extend' the seasons (global warming already promises us plenty of seasonal hiccups). We need, instead, to move closer to the seasons, to become more intuitive, to plan our growing better, and to be more realistic about just what we can or can't grow without the subsidy afforded by fossil fuels. With only a little experience we can 'stretch' the growing season by using cloches, polytunnels and unheated greenhouses – any structure that catches the sun's energy.

Can we really afford, financially, ecologically or morally, to be sowing tomato seeds in early February, just so we can pick fruits in June? Waiting another month won't bring us to our knees, and they'll probably taste better to boot. But our impatience to have our seeds sprinting into action, at the flick of a switch or the strike of a match, is helping to fuel the destruction of crops, in distant lands, on which life itself depends.

January 2007 – *Winner of the 2007 Garden Media Guild Environmental Award*

GREEN RESOLUTIONS

PEOPLE HAVE ME DOWN as a rather odd sort, and by sharing some of my New Year's resolutions I've managed to boost my 'raised eyebrow rating' to even dizzier heights. But I can't see much wrong with resolving to cut my 'garden centre miles', to put out patio heaters, or to challenge a wobbly Alan Titchmarsh on his continuing refusal to face up to the reality of global warming. Those are just some of my green resolutions for the gardening year that lies ahead.

It won't be difficult to cut my garden centre miles. Organically grown plants are still a rare sight in what have largely become little more than cathedrals to consumerism, so I rarely go plant-hunting there. The only way I can reliably get organically certified material is by mail order, which is how I usually obtain my organic seeds, too. So I seldom worship at a 'cathedral', other than to stock up on peat-free compost.

Buying seeds by mail order is an environmental winner. If ten people in your street buy their seeds by post, rather than during at least one visit to a garden centre, all ten orders will be delivered by the postie on his usual round. That's one vehicle (or push bike) journey that was being made anyway, as opposed to at least ten separate journeys, probably by car. The result is a dramatic reduction in garden centre miles and greenhouse gas emissions, more time to spend in the garden – and more chance of getting what you want.

But when I do find myself in a garden centre, another green-tinged resolution is to ask more questions. I'm going to start asking whether they stock any organically grown plants, and if not, why not. You might want to join me. My other questions will include whether they offer a home delivery service (one vehicle delivering to multiple addresses), whether they collect materials like plastics for recycling, and what proportion of their plants are home-grown or locally grown. I'd like to think that this year will be the one when gardeners everywhere start to think 'plant' as well as 'food' miles.

From plant miles, to air miles clocked up by... plants. I urge the Royal Horticultural Society (RHS), which organises Chelsea and the other big flower shows, to make this its New Year's resolution: to ban the flying in of plants, materials and people from the other side of the planet for a five-day wonder in late May. I'm hoping it will also announce a trugful of other green resolutions, such as a zero-waste policy at its shows, and more emphasis on public transport. Air travel is the most environmentally damaging form of transport on earth, so unless the top brass at the RHS have their heads in the compost heap, they'll put an end to encouraging the ecocidal madness of flying entire gardens through the air. At present, Chelsea is the most polluting, never mind the greatest, flower show on earth.

In contrast to the energy-guzzling that goes into making a national flower show, one of my greener resolutions is to grow more, using both less and more energy. I'm doing pretty well on the 'less' front; I don't use (or need) any powered gardening tools at all, apart from occasionally borrowing a shredder powered by renewable electricity. I won't be using any heated propagators either, so my energy conservation is looking pretty good. But where I'm resolving to start using much more energy is out in the garden. And no, I'm not going to start using patio heaters for frost protection. I'm going to start capturing energy by covering my soil in countless, living solar collectors – otherwise known as green manure crops.

The more I see these powerhouses in action, the more must-grow they become. Vegan-organic growers and gardeners have proved that you can build and sustain soil fertility using a combination of compost and green manures; you don't need farmyard manure mountains, ground-up dead animals, or energy-guzzling artificial fertilisers to get high yields of healthy crops. Why not resolve to trial the full range of green manures this year? Once you know what thrives, you can start giving your soil some added oomph. Just add sunlight.

The sun: if only we were more guided by its rising and setting, and by all of nature's daily, monthly and seasonal cycles. I recently had a close encounter in a garden centre with a flying saucer on a pole... a patio heater. Peering up into one of these things, it feels like an alien encounter is on the cards, and the idea that anyone would countenance the gardening equivalent of the 4x4 is even stranger than science fiction. The contribution that patio heaters make to global warming, just so we can sit outdoors chill-free instead of putting a thick coat on, sends a shudder down the spine.

We need to resolve to abandon the idea that we can go on gobbling finite fossil fuels, in the face of a near-complete consensus that human activity is dramatically altering the global climate. We should all resolve to challenge the use of patio heaters, whether it's a reasoned word with family, friends or neighbours, or a more robust approach to those peddling this contender for the most shameful and environmentally damaging 'gardening' invention of all time.

Talking of environmental damage, I do wonder just how much is being caused by the stance that some of our most influential celebrity gardeners choose to take. Last spring in *Organic Gardening* I questioned Alan Titchmarsh's flawed assertion that global warming isn't so much to do with human activity as with 'wobbles' affecting the earth's axis. Sadly Alan is still wobbling on what every other rational person knows; our own prime minister has called global warming 'not the greatest environmental threat, but the greatest threat' to our future. Writing in the November '06 issue of *Gardeners' World* magazine, Alan says, 'I don't doubt that the industrialisation of our planet has a bearing on our climate, and we must do everything within our power to keep such effects to a minimum. But to say how much we ourselves are affecting global warming can only be educated guesswork, and I've never been good at guessing.'

All I can guess is that Alan hasn't been reading the newspapers or watching the news for the past year, hasn't been to the cinema, hasn't read any of the well-researched books on the subject of climate change, and has no idea what the scientific evidence is. I wonder if he has a patio heater. My only hope is that he will make his own New Year's resolution to gen up on the dangers from unchecked global warming, and to stop clinging to the pathetic 'if experience has taught me anything it is that nothing is certain.'

What is certain is that a few words from Alan would be a hugely positive step in helping to reduce gardening's ecological footprint. In the case of patio heaters, for example, 'turn them off' would do nicely. *February 2007*

MAKE PESTICIDES HISTORY

IT'S A SAFE BET that a good proportion of readers of this magazine has, at one time or another, taken some kind of political action – even just by sending a lobbying postcard to your local councillor or MP. And you've probably added your voice to a call for something to be stopped, better regulated, or researched and scrutinised before being unleashed upon the world – genetically modified crops being a prime example.

So what sort of person do you think would pen the following, as they bemoan having to hand-pick caterpillars from their cabbages. 'In the past, one spray of the right systemic insecticide at the right time solved the problem. The loss of these chemicals is due to draconian and expensive EU testing regulations... But I will be writing to my MP.' Is this a flat-capped old curmudgeon who carpet-bombs his allotment with every pesticide under the sun, a novice plotter sold the 'if it moves, kill it' line, or a wishy-washy gardening celebrity spluttering, 'I only spray when I have to.'? The answer is none of the above.

These extraordinary comments were made on the pages of *Amateur Gardening* magazine, last autumn, by its editor. Just to avoid any doubt, Tim Rumball was writing to ask his MP to bring back garden chemicals which have been withdrawn under ever-tighter and increasingly planet-friendly legislation. The 'systemic' insecticides for which he pines are those that actually enter the sap stream of the plant. This means that they get right inside the plants' tissues and are absorbed into the leaves, flowers (including their pollen and nectar), roots and fruits.

The reasons for this sudden call to political action are limp. 'The withdrawal of many systemic insecticides leaves me with the options of covering everything with fleece, which looks horrible; using vast quantities of contact insecticides; or just putting up with serious damage to a lot of crops. I do not have time to hand-pick caterpillars...' Risking smugness, I think I have the answer to Tim's troubles: start gardening organically. It's got to be better than dousing your crops in man-made chemicals that get drawn into the heart of your crops – which you then put into your body.

We know that pesticide residues are commonplace in non-organic food, so it's astonishing that so many garden writers and commentators – and magazine editors – seem hell-bent on discrediting organics at every opportunity. Recent months have seen an increasing number of vitriolic and often incredibly ill-informed attacks on organic growing. I wonder why.

The stance of *Amateur Gardening* can easily be explained. Throughout the growing season last year it was plastered with advertisements for garden pesticides containing such chemicals as glyphosate and imidacloprid – both examples of the systemics which its editor craves. To quote Upton Sinclair, an American author and investigative journalist, 'It is difficult to get a man to understand something when his salary depends on his not understanding it.' This also sheds light on exactly why so many gardening celebrities remain vehemently non-committal on the subject of garden chemicals.

As awareness grows of the negative impacts that humanity is having on the ecosystems on which all life depends, it's mind-boggling that anyone would be batting for more garden pesticides. But their manufacturers are big beasts in the gardening industry, with plenty of clout – and money. I also have an inkling, despite much-trumpeted sales figures, that they are well and truly on the back foot. As organic gardeners we need to make sure they stay there – and preferably tip over backwards.

Being on the back foot might account for the virulent outpourings of perhaps our most un-green gardening writer, Peter Seabrook, who is as pro-pesticide, pro-peat and pro-GM as they come. Writing in his *Amateur Gardening* column in December 2006, he said, 'Organic is all very well for those of us either well off enough to pay the higher price or be prepared to grow our own and accept either more waste or lower yields... Growing organically at higher cost and with lower output is not an option for the majority.' More waste? Lower yields? Higher cost? It doesn't sound like the kind of organic gardening I know and love. I'm particularly intrigued as to what the higher costs of organic gardening are, given that we instinctively shun synthetic, energy-hungry fertilisers and pesticides, and have 'thrift' branded onto our tool handles.

But this naive sideswipe at organic gardening was merely camouflage for a more surreptitious plugging of, you guessed it, garden chemicals. Peter's piece is entitled 'Best of both worlds', and it explains the practice of Integrated Pest Management or IPM, a technique used by commercial growers which combines the use of naturally occurring bugs, bacteria and fungi with limited and carefully targeted pesticide use. It's a proven approach which works effectively – in the context of controlling pests and diseases affecting crops grown as large-scale monocultures, which as all good organic gardeners know is simply asking for problems.

There's no doubt that IPM is better than simply using pesticides as a matter of course, but the crafty aim of Peter's article was to discredit organics by implying that the only sensible way to grow is by using some chemicals. It allowed the magazine's front cover to shout out 'Organic + chemicals = success!', and it gave the editor a chance to rant, 'The 'don't' brigade annoy me – don't use a hose, don't use peat, don't use chemicals!', and to describe this apparently new frontier in pest and disease control as 'brilliant!'. I just can't help thinking that when pesticide residues are found in the bodies of species that have never been anywhere near our gardens, and when there are commercially proven alternatives to peat composts, it would seem only common sense to join the 'don't' brigade forthwith.

The most worrying and dangerous spin put on all of this is summed up by the caption below a picture of Peter Seabrook as he harvests lettuce. 'I prefer my lettuce and other produce without slugs, caterpillars and maggots so I'm prepared to use pesticides on my edible crops.' Peter obviously prefers the 'supermarket look' to slightly imperfect but residue-free.

Interest from people wanting to grow their own surged last year; edible seed and plant sales have rocketed, while celebrities are jostling to be the new kitchen garden 'expert'. This is largely good stuff, but be in no doubt that the chemical manufacturers are drooling even now as they eye up a new wave of gardeners who might help to shore up their flagging fortunes. I'm talking about enthusiasm-rich but knowledge-poor new gardeners, who are finding out the hard way that TV and magazine gardening is rather different from everyday reality, and who are being drip-fed the message that organic gardening is expensive, means maggots and gives poor returns.

Harsh reality and pesticide propaganda are a potent mix; the quick chemical fix has much allure for the vulnerable, and it'll be sold hard. As organic gardeners we need to expose the hollowness of gardening's spin-doctors, challenge wishy-washy celebrities, and grow true to our beliefs. By example and by cultivating 'greened-up thinking', we can make pesticides history. *March 2007*

DEAR PRESIDENT...

An open letter to the President of the
Royal Horticultural Society

Dear Peter Buckley,

How has your garden been these last few months? I imagine that, even up in Dumfriesshire, you've been wondering at times quite what the weather has been playing at. The warmest January since 1916 certainly had us gardeners pausing longer than usual as we gazed up to the heavens. Only hermits will be unaware of what's behind January's record-breaking temperatures – but as a gardener, I don't need a legion of the world's top climate change scientists to tell me that something's up; my worms are doing a grand job.

I'm talking about the worms in my compost bin. It's usually brimful around this time of year, and the worm equivalent of the Mary Celeste. They've normally shut up shop for the cold winter months – except that until the time of writing (the beginning of February), cold was absent. So my brandlings worked on through one of the warmest autumn spells recorded, and then on into January. Consequently, my bin is only around half full, thanks to unseasonal vermicultural overtime.

We both know that things like this shouldn't really be happening, and while I'm not turning my nose up at an early compost harvest, I am, along with other gardeners, growing increasingly concerned. But alongside that concern, I find an ever-strengthening resolve to not make matters any worse, and to do everything I can to put the brake on environmental meltdown. I feel oddly and deeply powerful. What I can do as an organic gardener is immense; my actions have a small but collectively positive effect on global ecosystems. Although stuff like switching off those blessed stand-by buttons is important, it pales in comparison with organic gardening.

I'm writing to you both as a fellow gardener and as President of the Royal Horticultural Society (RHS). 'The UK's leading gardening charity dedicated to advancing horticulture and promoting good gardening' has some 360,000 paid-up members, me included. The concerns I mentioned earlier come rushing back the moment I try to balance my RHS member's hat on top of my organic one – it's like trying to stack square pots with round ones.

A lot has been said about climate systems reaching a 'tipping point', spurred on by greenhouse gases. Well, I've just reached my own tipping point, after reading on the RHS website that in a few months' time, the Chelsea Flower Show will feature yet another garden flown in from the far side of the planet – Australia to be precise. At least it's not as bad as last year, when one came over from New Zealand too. With all the coverage of global warming since last year's Chelsea, including much discussion of the serious damage done by aircraft emissions, I half hoped the RHS might have joined the mushrooming awareness of 'green' issues by announcing that it no longer considers that flying plants and materials from the other side of the world to be ecologically – or morally – sustainable. After all, damaging climate change is already a reality in some parts of the world, and it's killing people.

Looking on your website at the RHS's five-year plan for 2006 to 2010, this aim leaps out: 'To practice and promote environmental [*sic*] responsible horticulture and gardening', along with mention of the creation of 'long-term environmental improvements'. Would you agree that one way the RHS can promote such improvements, and show it is in tune with the times, is to end the potty idea of air-freighting gardens in from overseas, for a lifespan of a mere five days?

Our big national flower shows are an ecological conundrum. They consume vast amounts of energy in their build-up and breakdown and generate mountains of waste (I don't need to tell you that Chelsea is like Skip City before it opens) – and that's just putting the infrastructure together. When you start factoring in the catering waste generated by a major flower show (you only get real/reusable glasses in the posh bits), not to mention the local surge in vehicle pollution (stuck on the M6 trying to get into Tatton), it makes your toes curl. Upwards. Let's face it, the huge ecological footprint stomped on the planet by Chelsea and its ilk is nowhere near justified by the handful of practical and realistic gardening ideas that a visitor might glean from a show.

Now I'm sure you've got the best brains in the RHS working on all this stuff, but I'd like to throw in a few suggestions of my own. Firstly, how about linking ticket price to the means of travelling to a show? Essentially, visitors arriving by public transport would pay considerably less (if they arrive by push bike, I'd let them in for free). You would therefore reward gardeners who left their cars at home and did their bit to reduce greenhouse gas emissions. You'd certainly earn greenie points with me. As for the vast amounts of electricity which have to be generated on site, and the vehicle fuel required, renewably-generated electricity, biodiesel and other 'greener' fuels are available. How about using them? – a great chance here to announce, 'RHS flower shows go green!'

That's energy and transport sorted, but what about all those skips overflowing with catering waste? If sandwiches really must come in triangular packs, can't you insist that the packs are made of compostable corn starch? Marks & Spencer do it now. In fact, why not insist that the RHS show caterers use entirely recyclable/ compostable materials and, to ice the cake, demand they source only organic and local ingredients?

If you fancy deepest green, how about making the RHS shows 'carbon neutral'? Yes, it'll involve some number crunching to work out a show's overall emissions of greenhouse gases, but just think how it will inform the way you put on these big shows in the future – if indeed they remain tenable in the long term. It might mean a hefty ticket price rise, but shouldn't we be paying the true environmental cost?

You know, I think the idea of charging visitors according to their means of travel could also work a treat at your regional gardens. I visited Harlow Carr in Yorkshire last summer. As a member, I got in free – but any non-member who travelled, like me, by public transport still paid the same entry fee as those arriving by car. This kind of incentive would surely boost visitor numbers and encourage improved public transport links (only one bus a day linking Wisley with the local train station?), while the ecological footprints left by visitors to RHS gardens would become some of the lightest around. But why stop there? How about making all of the RHS gardens, indeed the entire organisation, carbon neutral? It's quite a thought.

My worms are now well and truly in winter recess. This part of Snowdonia fell to -10°C the other night, so everything's back to normal. At least for now. I hope my musings are helpful, and I look forward to getting some feedback on my ideas and your answers to my questions.

Until then, I wish you a successful gardening season, whatever climatic surprises it may bring us.

Sustainably yours,
John Walker
(No reply was ever received.) *April 2007*

RELATIVE MERITS

ORGANIC GARDENING has a problem, and it's called organic farming. You might think that there is an indisputable and natural synergy between the two, and of course you'd be right. They work to shared sets of beliefs, principles and practices, and generally there's a healthy flow of information and knowledge between home gardeners, allotment holders, smallholders and organic farmers. Back in the days when the bigger commercial growers were dipping their toes in the organic market, I clearly remember being struck by how the wisest words came from those with modest smallholdings and small organic farms. Small was (and still is) beautiful.

Now 'organic', in all its forms, is big – big business, big profits, big news. The Soil Association (SA) reports a 30% increase in sales of organic goods in 2006, in a UK 'organic industry' worth £1.6 billion. We could debate whether industrialisation, and especially the industrialisation of organic farming, is actually good news. But the fact that organic farming now hits the headlines regularly, and not always in a positive light, is turning out to be unequivocally bad news for organic gardeners.

The most recent example of how we gardeners run the risk of being trashed by association came in February this year. 'Organic farming 'no better for the environment'', cried the headline. The article started, 'Organic food may be no better for the environment than conventional produce and in some cases is contributing more to global warming than intensive agriculture, according to a government report.' This was hot on the heels of the suggestion, made a few weeks earlier by the Environment Secretary David Miliband, that organic food was a 'lifestyle choice'.

On the face of it, neither story was exactly 'good news' for organics, although the SA did release an effective rebuttal of the government report's findings, describing some of its conclusions as 'irrelevant'. And Miliband did recant, admitting that organic farming was better for the environment, although he maintains there is no proof of health benefits from this 'choice'. But the damage has been done, giving the pro-chemical harpies circling the 'o' word even more to flap about.

Last autumn I took part in a radio phone-in for BBC Radio Kent's Sunday gardening programme. The focus was organics and, you would have thought, organic gardening in particular. But oh no, we were soon off at a tangent, ably guided by the programme's resident gardening 'expert', with the guest from the SA being grilled over claims that so-called 'midnight sprayers' somewhere in Spain were undermining the certification of organic produce, if not the entire organic movement. Claims, incidentally, that the resident expert had 'heard about' while in Europe, and which the beleaguered SA person was therefore unable to comment on directly.

Result? The programme got off to a flying start by giving organics, and by association organic gardening, a good kicking. Impression given? 'Organics' is a scam selling overpriced food with meaningless labels, so organic gardening must be part of the con. Sorted. It's manna for the bashers of organic gardening, who'll use every trick in the book to undermine what we're doing out on our plots. This latest rash of 'bad news days' for organics must have the pro-chemical crowd drooling some of the 4.5 billion litres of pesticides slopped onto UK crops every year.

But surely people understand the difference between organic farming and organic gardening? I'm not so sure that they do. I think many people don't see a difference, despite the fact that the term 'organic' is lodged in our collective consciousness, regardless of whether or not we choose to eat, wear or grow it. So when organic farming is given a pummelling in the media, organic gardening gets a winding as well.

But to use the apparent ills and inevitable shortcomings of organic farming to smear organic gardening is a travesty. Those who do, and who will continue to try to get us squirming, urgently need a reality check. So, just for them, here's a potted version of the difference between the two (you can add to my list, ready for the next time you encounter an ill-informed ignoramus on the radio or elsewhere).

Organic gardening incurs minimal or zero 'food miles'; our growing is as local as it gets. The SA is currently debating whether food grown organically, then shipped in from the far side of the planet, should actually be certified as organic (answer probably no). We gardeners are already well ahead of both organic and conventional farming on that score. Our distance-ometer ranges from food inches as we gather herbs from the window box, to at worst a couple of food miles if our allotments are beyond the range of walking, cycling or public transport.

Organic gardening requires no packaging, and so no energy and raw materials are needed to make, print, transport and dispose of packaging. We don't even need the ink to print the logos identifying our produce as organic. And we can sleep easy knowing that by eliminating packaging, we're not helping to build plastic mountains in China, where much of our 'recycling' now ends up.

Organic gardening uses no synthetic, energy- and material-hungry artificial fertilisers or pesticides, fungicides or weedkillers. Organic farmers can still use a very restricted range of substances approved for organic use, so we gardeners are ahead of the game here too if we avoid the organic 'quick fixes' and instead harmonise our garden ecosystems. So we have no need of packaging on this score either, nor of the energy-guzzling transport that would be required to get the stuff to us.

Organic gardening proudly flaunts the message that 'small is beautiful'; it works on a relatively small scale, while creating barely any environmental footprint. In contrast, organic farming is, on the whole, becoming ever larger-scale. To keep supermarket shelves stocked, even with organic produce, you need lots of it, and of the specified size, shape and quality. We gardeners can live with things being different in size or misshapen, and we don't usually mind a blemish here, or an aphid there.

Organic gardening is about creating vibrant, diverse ecosystems which enrich their surroundings. It helps to build soil and, by using the no-dig or minimal cultivation approach, it increases soil carbon content, so helping to check climate change. It improves both our physical and our spiritual health, and that of planetary ecosystems. It recaptures a growing sense of the self-reliance so frighteningly absent from current generations. When our fingers hit the soil, we reconnect with where we've actually come from.

It gives me goosebumps every time I think just how many of the 'sustainable living' boxes the gentle act of organic gardening actually ticks. Yet so very often, whenever the organic bashers grab their cudgel, it has the organic farming label dangling from it. There's no doubt that organic farming has its own demons to face, as growing demand for organic food nudges it towards industrial-scale production, but organic gardening is very different. If we're ranking on the basis of how environmentally sound and 'earth-friendly' something is, I'd say organic gardeners were on the top spot. We should not be tarred with the same brush. *May 2007*

A good read?

Without reviews from readers like you, it's hard to spread the word about independently published books like this one, and help them reach more readers.

Leaving an honest review in the online store where you bought the book only takes a few minutes and it doesn't have to be long or complicated; just a few sentences sharing with other gardeners what you liked about *Digging Deep in the Garden: Book One*, and what they might like about it themselves, would be incredibly valuable to me.

In truth, very few readers leave book reviews. Adding yours helps me, as an independent, self-publishing writer, to sell more earth-friendly gardening books – and to create new ones.

Thank you.

Why not enjoy another good read?

To be among the first to hear about forthcoming books in the *Digging Deep in the Garden* series, as well as other publications from Earth-friendly Books, you can sign up, safely and securely, for my occasional newsletter (sent by email) by visiting www.earthfriendlygardener.net and following the newsletter sign-up instructions.

Comments or observations on my books are always welcome. Please email john@earthfriendlygardener.net, or join me on Twitter @earthFgardener

About John Walker

John Walker is an award-winning gardening and environmental author, writer, blogger and publisher with 40 years' experience in practical gardening, teaching and the garden media. He grew up in the countryside, caught the gardening bug while still at school, and trained at Birmingham Botanical Gardens, Cambridge University Botanic Garden and the Royal Botanic Gardens Kew, where he was awarded the Kew Diploma in Horticulture. He is also a qualified teacher. John was features/deputy editor of *Garden Answers* magazine and contributing editor of *Kitchen Garden*.

John writes about organic, earth-friendly gardening for national newspapers and magazines, including *The Guardian* and *The Daily Telegraph* and the Royal Horticultural Society's journal *The Garden*. His recent book *How to Create an Eco Garden: The Practical Guide to Greener, Planet-friendly Gardening* was shortlisted for the 2012 Garden Media Guild Practical Book of the Year. He also wrote *The Bed and Border Planner* and *Weeds: An Organic, Earth-friendly Guide to their Identification, Use and Control*, edited *A Gardeners' Guide to Annuals*, and contributed to the *Garden Organic Encyclopedia of Organic Gardening*. John has won the Garden Media Guild Environmental Award three times, and has been shortlisted for Gardening Journalist of the Year three times.

John is slowly making a new earth- and climate-friendly garden from a once bracken-riddled hillside at his edge-of-woodland home in Snowdonia, North Wales.

Visit John's website www.earthfriendlygardener.net, follow him on Twitter at @earthFgardener, or email john@earthfriendlygardener.net

Printed in Great Britain
by Amazon.co.uk, Ltd.,
Marston Gate.